Original title:
The Friendship File

Copyright © 2024 Swan Charm
All rights reserved.

Author: Johan Kirsipuu
ISBN HARDBACK: 978-9916-86-578-1
ISBN PAPERBACK: 978-9916-86-579-8
ISBN EBOOK: 978-9916-86-580-4

The Language of Trust

In whispered words, a bond takes flight,
A silent pact, in day and night.
Eyes that speak, no need for sound,
In gentle gestures, love is found.

Through laughter shared and sorrows spilled,
Each promise made, each heart fulfilled.
The hands that hold, the hearts that dare,
In trust we weave, a love so rare.

Gossamer Threads

Delicate strands that shimmer and sway,
Binding souls in a tender ballet.
With every touch, they softly glide,
In the dance of life, side by side.

Through stormy nights and sunny days,
These threads of love weave intricate ways.
In the fabric of time, they gently twine,
A masterpiece crafted, distinctly divine.

Moments Captured

Fleeting glances, seconds freeze,
In laughter's echo, memories tease.
With every heartbeat, time stands still,
In cherished moments, we find our will.

From whispered secrets to shared delight,
Each captured breath ignites the night.
In the gallery of hearts, we frame,
The beauty of love, never the same.

A Haven in His Presence

In quiet corners where shadows lay,
A haven blooms at the end of day.
With open arms, the heart will find,
Peace and solace, intertwined.

In his presence, worries cease,
A gentle whisper brings sweet release.
Together we breathe in the stillness near,
In this sanctuary, love draws near.

In the Company of Hearts

In quiet whispers, we confide,
Two souls dancing, side by side.
With every glance, a secret shared,
In the warmth, we are prepared.

Time flows softly, like a stream,
Together woven, like a dream.
Through laughter sweet and sting of tears,
We gather strength and face our fears.

In stormy nights, we find our grace,
With tender hands, we embrace space.
The world fades away, just we two,
In the company, hearts so true.

Music of Familiarity

In every note, a tale unfolds,
A melody of warmth and gold.
Familiar rhythms fill the air,
A dance of memories laid bare.

The strum of strings, a gentle call,
Echoes of laughter, rise and fall.
In harmony, our hearts align,
An orchestra where souls combine.

With whispers soft, the night ignites,
In every sound, our love excites.
Together we create the score,
The music of us, forevermore.

The Art of Unspoken Words

In silence deep, the truth does dwell,
A glance, a smile, hearts compelled.
The language shared without a sound,
In moments small, our love is found.

With fingers brush, a spark ignites,
A touch that lingers, soft delights.
In spaces filled with tender sighs,
Our souls converse, no need for lies.

Each pause a canvas, vast and wide,
Where love paints colors, deep inside.
In every sigh, the world is heard,
The beauty found in unspoken word.

Light in the Shadows

In twilight's arms, the shadows creep,
Yet light breaks through, a promise deep.
With every dawn, new hope is born,
In darkest times, we are not torn.

Through hidden paths, we learn to see,
The strength in light, the way to be.
With every step, the shadows fade,
In courage's glow, we are remade.

As stars align in midnight's breath,
We find the light that conquers death.
In every heart, a spark ignites,
A beacon shining through the nights.

Echoes of Togetherness

In the quietude of night,
Laughter dances in the air,
Memories twinkle like stars,
Binding hearts with gentle care.

Through the storms, we shall stand,
Hands united, strong and true,
In the echoes of our whispers,
A symphony of me and you.

Time may chase us from our dreams,
But friendship holds its ground tight,
In the echoes, we shall linger,
Together, our souls take flight.

Paths may twist and turn away,
Yet our bond won't break or bend,
Through the valleys and the peaks,
Together, we shall always mend.

In the tapestry of moments,
Threads of gold we weave and share,
In the echoes of togetherness,
Love's melody fills the air.

Heartstrings Entwined

Two souls in the quiet dusk,
Find their rhythm in the night,
Strings of hearts begin to hum,
In the glow of soft moonlight.

With every glance, a spark ignites,
A song that only we can hear,
In the silence, whispers bloom,
Binding you and I so near.

Through the trials that we face,
Our hearts dance in perfect sync,
With every joy and every tear,
We delve deeper, never think.

Hand in hand, we wander wide,
Through life's maze, we find our way,
In the bond that time creates,
Love's notes in bright array.

Together in this symphony,
A melody forever true,
In the heartstrings, gently pulled,
Life's sweetest song is me and you.

Whispers of Loyalty

In the shadows, whispers dwell,
Soft and steadfast in the night,
A promise forged in silence,
Wrapped in loyalty's soft light.

Through the trials, we won't waver,
Side by side, we brave the storm,
In our hearts, a seal unbroken,
Through the dark, we keep each warm.

Like the roots of ancient trees,
Our bond runs deep below the ground,
In whispers soft, we find our strength,
In loyalty, true love is found.

Moments shared, both small and grand,
Echo in the fabric we create,
With each trust, the whispers grow,
In the circle of love's estate.

Together we stand, hand in hand,
Through the echoes, strong and free,
In whispers of loyalty's song,
Forever, it will be you and me.

Canvas of Kindred Souls

Brush strokes of laughter and tears,
Color the canvas of our days,
In hues of joy and moments shared,
We paint our life in vibrant ways.

With every dawn, a new design,
Every sunset, a shade of gold,
In the tapestry of our spirits,
The stories of our hearts unfold.

Kindred souls in this great art,
Creating beauty with each breath,
As the colors blend so softly,
Life's masterpiece conquers death.

Through storms and sunny weather,
With strokes of courage, we create,
A canvas rich with memories,
A portrait of our shared fate.

In the gallery of our lives,
Every moment, a treasure trove,
On the canvas, forever bound,
In the art of love, we move.

Crossroads of Connection

At the crossroads, paths entwine,
Two souls meet, a spark divine.
In silence shared, they find their way,
Unspoken words begin to play.

With every glance, a story grows,
A dance of fate, as the river flows.
Hands reach out, a bridge is formed,
Through whispered hope, a bond is warmed.

Life spins on, yet time stands still,
Moments captured, hearts to fill.
In every twist, a choice to make,
Together strong, no fear to shake.

Seasons change, yet they remain,
In the storm, through joy and pain.
At the crossroads, love will thrive,
In unity, they come alive.

As paths diverge, they hold a thread,
A tapestry of words unsaid.
At this junction, a world is spun,
Two souls as one, a journey begun.

Cherished Footprints

In the sands of time, footprints lie,
Each one tells a tale, a sigh.
Memories etched beneath the sun,
Whispers of journeys, now begun.

With every step, a path unfolds,
In laughter shared, and secrets told.
Footprints fading, yet hearts will stay,
In cherished moments, never stray.

Through fields of gold and skies of blue,
Every trail leads back to you.
In timeless echoes, love's embrace,
We find our home, our sacred space.

Rain may wash the marks away,
Yet in my heart, they softly lay.
A map of love, both deep and wide,
In cherished footprints, we confide.

Together wandering, hand in hand,
Forever bound to this blessed land.
In each print, our story's penned,
With every step, love knows no end.

Heartbeats in Sync

In quiet moments, two hearts beat,
A rhythm shared, a steady heat.
In gentle whispers, a bond is cast,
With every pulse, the die is cast.

Life's melody, a song so sweet,
Each heartbeat echoes, a dance complete.
In perfect harmony, they align,
With every thump, the stars resign.

Through trials faced and laughter shared,
In every heartbeat, love declared.
A symphony of souls in flight,
Together painting day and night.

When shadows fall and fears arise,
Their heartbeats soar to meet the skies.
In unity, they find their way,
In every pulse, a brightened day.

Through every heartbeat, they remain,
In sync forever, joy and pain.
A fiery dance, a sacred link,
In purest love, their spirits sink.

Gathering of Kindred Spirits

Underneath the starlit sky,
Kindred souls begin to sigh.
In shared laughter, hearts unite,
A gathering of warmth, delight.

With every tale, they weave a thread,
Of experiences, tears, and bread.
In circles drawn, connections grow,
As ancient bonds begin to flow.

Together spinning stories bright,
The past and present, pure delight.
In every smile, a spark ignites,
In every moment, joy ignites.

Through seasons changing, they stand strong,
In heart and spirit, where they belong.
Together facing life's grand scheme,
In kindred spirits, they dream.

As time unveils, they're ever near,
A melody that all will hear.
In unity, they lift the night,
A gathering of love, pure light.

Echoes of Laughter

In the garden where we played,
Joyful shouts and dreams conveyed.
Sunlight danced on faces bright,
Echoes linger in the night.

Laughter weaves through memories clear,
Whispers soft that we hold dear.
Every smile a thread entwined,
In the heart, their warmth we find.

Moments captured, forever stored,
In the light, our spirits soared.
Together we embraced the day,
In laughter's arms, we chose to stay.

Through storms and trials, joys arise,
In laughter, we see the skies.
Echoes fade but never die,
In our hearts, they learn to fly.

So let us dance in sweet delight,
As echoes linger in the night.
For every laugh we tossed above,
Is a reminder of our love.

Paths Intertwined

Two paths crossed on a quiet morn,
Each step forward, new lives born.
With shared dreams and whispered hopes,
Together, through the unseen slopes.

Moments shared, journeys begun,
Underneath the golden sun.
Hand in hand through thick and thin,
A bond forged from within.

In laughter's glow and shadows cast,
We found a love that's built to last.
With every turn and gentle sway,
Paths entwined in perfect play.

Through every challenge that we face,
We carve our way with steady grace.
Hearts beating in a timeless rhyme,
Together we surpass all time.

So let us walk this road so true,
In every shade, in every hue.
With trust as our guiding star,
In this dance, we'll never part.

Heartfelt Happenings

In quiet moments shared with you,
Every heartbeat feels so true.
Whispers soft like gentle rain,
Echoing love, dispelling pain.

Time suspends in tender grace,
As I gaze upon your face.
Every laugh, every sigh,
Creates a world where dreams can fly.

From sunset hues to dawn's embrace,
Life unfolds at a perfect pace.
In every joy, in every tear,
Heartfelt happenings draw us near.

With hands entwined, our story grows,
In every challenge, love still glows.
We weave a tale of brave delight,
In heartfelt happenings, we unite.

So here's to moments rich and rare,
A tapestry beyond compare.
Together, we can stand as one,
In every heartbeat, we have won.

Secrets in the Circle

In shadows cast where whispers dwell,
Secrets form a sacred shell.
In the circle, trust takes flight,
An unbroken bond, pure and bright.

With every word that softly flows,
In quiet corners, friendship grows.
Underneath the silvered sky,
We share our dreams, we laugh, we cry.

In these moments, time stands still,
With open hearts, we dare to spill.
Every secret bears a weight,
In the circle, we celebrate.

Through fear and doubt, we stand as one,
In unity, we've just begun.
With hands held tight, we face it all,
In the circle, we're never small.

So let us gather, voices strong,
In this circle where we belong.
For every secret shared in trust,
Builds the love that's more than just.

Journeys of the Heart

Across the winding roads we roam,
Seeking the place that feels like home.
With every step, the stories grow,
In whispers of love, our spirits flow.

Through valleys deep and mountains high,
We chase the dreams that lift us sky.
Hand in hand, we face the night,
Our hearts in sync, a guiding light.

With every beat, a promise made,
In trials faced, we will not fade.
Together strong, we'll brave the storm,
In the warmth of love, we find our form.

The oceans vast will not divide,
In every wave, our hopes collide.
Through every tear, a lesson learned,
For in our hearts, the fire burns.

Each journey shared brings us closer,
A tapestry of joy, no poser.
In laughter's echo, we find our tune,
Our hearts will sing beneath the moon.

Bonds Beyond Time

In every glance, a story lies,
Invisible threads that never die.
Through laughter shared and silence kept,
In shadows cast, our secrets wept.

Across the ages, we intertwine,
In dreams and hopes, our stars align.
With every heartbeat, a song is sung,
In voices low, our souls are young.

Though distance stretches, we're still near,
In whispered thoughts that we can hear.
With every moment, we bridge the gap,
With love as fuel, our worlds overlap.

In photographs and faded notes,
Our memories float like gentle boats.
Through time, our laughter echoes still,
In every moment, we feel the thrill.

With every touch, we weave a lore,
In every hug, we cherish more.
Together we rise, though apart we tread,
In bonds that flourish, love is spread.

Palettes of Memory

Each brushstroke holds a tale untold,
In vibrant hues, the past unfolds.
With colors bright and shadows deep,
In art we find what dreams can keep.

In sunsets painted with golden light,
We cherish moments that feel so right.
With every scene, nostalgia swells,
In canvases, our heart's farewell.

The palette shifts as seasons change,
In every shade, a world rearranged.
Through autumn leaves to winter's chill,
In each transition, we feel the thrill.

In whispers of spring and summer's blaze,
Our memories linger in joyful haze.
With brush in hand, we capture time,
In every stroke, a rhythm, a rhyme.

As stories blend, their colors mix,
In life's grand tapestry, we fix.
Through art and heart, our journeys flow,
In palettes of memory, we eternally grow.

Connections in Bloom

In gardens lush, where friendships thrive,
The seeds of kindness come alive.
With every smile, new blossoms break,
In fragrant whispers, the world we make.

Through sunlight's touch and gentle rain,
In every heart, love conquers pain.
As petals unfold beneath the sky,
Together we reach, and we learn to fly.

The roots entwined beneath the earth,
In silent strength, we find our worth.
With every challenge, we rise as one,
In harmony, we dance, we run.

As seasons change and flowers fade,
The bonds we share will never trade.
In memory's garden, we left our mark,
With vibrant dreams igniting the spark.

So let us bloom, our colors shine,
In every moment, your heart in mine.
With love as soil, we'll grow anew,
In connections forged, forever true.

The Invisible Thread

In silence, whispers weave a tale,
A bond unseen, yet strong as rail.
Hearts entwined by fate's gentle hand,
An echo in the vast, uncharted land.

Each glance a spark, each touch a thread,
In the tapestry of moments fed.
Time may drift, like clouds in flight,
Yet love remains, a guiding light.

Through storms that rage and shadows cast,
The thread endures, holding fast.
With every laugh, with every sigh,
It stretches wide, it reaches high.

In quiet spaces, it softly hums,
A melody where true love comes.
Though paths may part and seasons change,
The invisible thread will rearrange.

So trust the pull, the gentle sway,
For connections linger, come what may.
In hearts entwined, forever shown,
The invisible thread, a love well-known.

Sheltering Arms

Beneath the stormy skies of grey,
A refuge found where shadows play.
In arms that wrap like twilight mist,
A warm embrace where fears desist.

With every heartbeat, comfort flows,
As petals fall from wilting rose.
The world outside may clash and roar,
Yet here, we find what we adore.

Each whisper shared, a soothing balm,
In tender moments, we feel calm.
A fortress built with love's embrace,
Where worries vanish, pains efface.

Through laughter bright and sorrows shared,
In every challenge, love has dared.
So let the winds of change arise,
In sheltering arms, our spirits rise.

Together woven, souls entwined,
In this sanctuary, peace we find.
A haven warm, forever strong,
In sheltering arms, we both belong.

The Alchemy of Affection

In moments small, we shape the gold,
Through each kind word, love's story told.
With gentle hands, we craft the fate,
The alchemy of hearts that wait.

A spark ignites, a tender glance,
Transforming silence into dance.
In laughter's glow and soothing tone,
We blend our souls, we're not alone.

Like starlight scattered, dreams take flight,
With every touch, we spark the night.
The simmering joy, the deepening trust,
In love's embrace, we find our must.

Through every trial, through every tear,
Alchemy of affection draws us near.
In the crucible of life's sweet fight,
Our spirits merge, igniting light.

So raise a glass to this pure art,
For every change begins the heart.
In every moment, joy's reflection,
We find the magic of affection.

Stories Untold

In shadows deep where secrets lie,
Whispers weave through the night sky.
Unwritten tales of love and pain,
In every heart, a silver chain.

Each glance a chapter yet to be,
Moments lost in reverie.
The stories echo, softly call,
In silent rooms, in memories' thrall.

Through laughter shared and tears that fall,
Life unfolds its grandest sprawl.
Every heartbeat, every sigh,
Shapes the tales that never die.

With every journey, paths entwine,
The stories grow through space and time.
For in each life, a seed is sown,
In stories untold, we find our own.

So gather round, let voices soar,
In every heart, there's so much more.
In pages blank, let dreams unfold,
The magic lies in stories untold.

Tapestry of Togetherness

In every thread, our stories weave,
Laughter shared, hearts believe.
Colors blend, no shades apart,
Stitched with love, a timeless art.

Through trials faced, we stand as one,
Chasing dreams beneath the sun.
Hands united, we'll find our way,
In this tapestry, we'll forever stay.

The fabric strong, yet soft to touch,
Weighted by care, it means so much.
Together we rise, never alone,
In this bond, we've found our home.

With every glance, a spark ignites,
Together we share our joys and plights.
Stitches of hope, crafted with care,
In this art, we'll always share.

A tapestry rich, with memories bright,
Woven in day, embraced in night.
Each thread a promise, steadfast and true,
In every color, a love renewed.

Silent Echoes of Support

In hushed tones, we stand side by side,
A bond unspoken, nothing to hide.
Through whispered fears, we share the load,
In silent echoes, our strength bestowed.

Amidst the chaos, a calming breath,
With every heartbeat, we conquer death.
A nod, a smile, understanding flows,
In quiet moments, our comfort grows.

Through darkest nights, we shine a light,
Guiding each other, holding tight.
No words need speak, our hearts declare,
In silence deep, we show we care.

Together we rise, against the tide,
With gentle courage, we will abide.
When storms may rage, we find our calm,
In silent echoes, we are the balm.

Through life's ups and its unseen downs,
With silent strength, we wear the crowns.
Each heartbeat echoes, firm and still,
In quiet support, we find our will.

Unseen Ties

Invisible threads bind us close,
In every gaze, our hearts engross.
A delicate dance, in shadow and light,
Unseen ties that feel so right.

Through laughter's note and silence shared,
In every moment, love is declared.
A gentle pull, a subtle embrace,
In unseen ties, we find our place.

Across the miles, our hearts align,
In thoughts as whispers, we intertwine.
Invisible bonds, so true and pure,
In every heartbeat, we're reassured.

Through storms and calm, we draw near,
In unseen ties, we hold what's dear.
In every challenge, together we rise,
With unseen ties, our spirits fly.

Forever linked, through time and space,
In threads unbroken, we find our grace.
Wherever we roam, our hearts still sing,
In unseen ties, love's eternal spring.

Mosaic of Moments

In pieces bright, life's moments shine,
Each fragment captured, a story divine.
A patchwork quilt of joy and pain,
In this mosaic, we dance in the rain.

Colors blend, each hue unique,
In every smile, we find the peek.
Fragments cherished, sewn with care,
A mosaic grows, a love affair.

Through fleeting glances and tender days,
We gather memories in wondrous ways.
A swirl of laughter, a sprinkle of tears,
In this mosaic, we quiet our fears.

Moments dance, like leaves in the breeze,
In every heartbeat, life's joyful tease.
Together we paint this life of ours,
A mosaic aglow, under the stars.

Each piece a chapter, woven so tight,
In this tapestry of shared light.
With every fragment, we tell our tale,
In this mosaic, we will prevail.

Sunlight on a Grey Day

Clouds gather, shadows play,
Yet a spark lights the way.
Warm rays break through the dim,
Hope arises, strong and slim.

In silence, whispers bloom,
Defying the encroaching gloom.
A soft glow, heart's delight,
Chasing away the night.

Gentle breezes start to sway,
Bringing laughter, come what may.
Each beam, a tender sigh,
Promises in the sky.

As raindrops gently fall,
Nature's rhythm, a calling thrall.
Embracing warmth, I find,
Joy that dances in my mind.

Through grey days and bright,
Sunlight brings a tender sight.
Each flicker a soft embrace,
In its warmth, I find my place.

The Warmth of a Kindred Spirit

In the quiet of our hearts,
Two souls drift, never apart.
A glance shared, a knowing smile,
Together we could walk each mile.

Laughter shared, like honey sweet,
In comfort found, our souls greet.
Through thick and thin, we will stand,
Together, life feels so grand.

Every story, old and new,
Each secret, whispered true.
Kindred hearts, a bond so tight,
In shared moments, pure delight.

When shadows stretch, and nights are long,
In your presence, I am strong.
The warmth of you, my guiding star,
No matter where, no matter far.

Forever friends, in joy and pain,
A love that will forever remain.
In the tapestry of our days,
Together we weave the brightest ways.

Colorful Connections

In a world of hues so bright,
Friendship dances, pure delight.
With every laugh and tear we share,
Colors intertwine, love laid bare.

The red of passion, hearts aflame,
Sunny yellows, joy we claim.
Greens of growth in every glance,
Blue horizons, a hopeful dance.

Each shade tells a story true,
Of moments shared and bonds we grew.
From darkest nights, the stars appear,
A palette rich, where hearts draw near.

In every splatter, art unfolds,
In colors bright, our tale is told.
With brush and strokes, we paint our way,
In vibrant shades, we seize the day.

Together, we make a canvas whole,
Where every color touches the soul.
In this garden, love takes flight,
Colorful connections, pure and bright.

Ribbons of Affection

Tied with care, a ribbon gold,
In every loop, a story told.
With soft threads, we weave our dreams,
In every glance, affection gleams.

Across the miles, they gently sway,
Binding hearts in a heartfelt way.
A twinkling touch, a sweet caress,
In tangled love, we find our rest.

The knot of trust, strong and clear,
In times of joy and of fear.
Colors bright, our spirits soar,
With every knot, we love even more.

These ribbons hold the warmth we share,
A tapestry with threads laid bare.
Unraveled tales of hearts so free,
Interwoven, you and me.

In every fold, a promise made,
In every twist, affection laid.
Together, we dance, a woven song,
Ribbons of love, where we belong.

The Bridge Between Us

A gentle path that we both tread,
Under stars that softly spread.
With every step, hand in hand,
Together we take a loving stand.

Whispers float on evening air,
In this bond, we lay our care.
Through storms and sun, we learn to see,
The bridge of trust, you and me.

Time may shift like the tide's pull,
Yet our hearts remain so full.
In every laugh and every tear,
You are the voice I hold dear.

Mountains high, valleys low,
Our spirits rise, together they glow.
Each memory, a stone we place,
Building a world, a sacred space.

And when shadows start to creep,
In the silence, promises we keep.
We find the light in what we share,
A bridge that flourishes with care.

Seasons of Loyalty

Winter whispers, cold and bright,
Bringing warmth on frosty nights.
In every snowflake, a secret lies,
Trust blooms where the heart never dies.

Spring awakens the sleeping earth,
Renewing our bond, showing its worth.
Petals unfold, carrying the tune,
Of loyalty grounded, beneath the moon.

Summer's laughter, a joyful song,
Together we dance, where we belong.
Sunlight warms an open heart,
In this season, we never part.

Autumn's colors paint the trees,
Falling leaves, a gentle breeze.
Through change and growth, our spirits soar,
Seasons of loyalty, forevermore.

In every phase, your hand in mine,
Together we flourish, truly divine.
Through storms and sunlight, we'll endure,
In loyalty's glow, our hearts are pure.

The Quilt of Friendship

Each patch a story, stitched with care,
Threads of laughter, memories rare.
In every square, love takes its place,
A quilt of friendship, a warm embrace.

Colors vibrant, woven tight,
In storms we find our shared light.
Every tear turns to a seam,
Creating warmth from a shared dream.

Over time, the fabric wears,
Yet our bond deepens, love declares.
In fragile moments, we stand strong,
The quilt of friendship, where we belong.

Together we gather under its fold,
Tales of courage and hearts bold.
In quiet whispers, laughter's sound,
In this tapestry, we are bound.

Through seasons shifting, patterns change,
Yet in our hearts, it feels the same.
Crafted by time, it's safe and true,
The quilt of friendship, me and you.

Echoes in the Quiet

In the stillness, whispers dwell,
Messages only hearts can tell.
Soft echoes fill the tranquil night,
As dreams take wing, taking flight.

Moments linger like a gentle breeze,
Carrying hopes with perfect ease.
In the quiet, we find our song,
Resonance where we both belong.

Memories fade, but love stays clear,
In every echo, you draw near.
Through silence thick, our voices blend,
In whispers shared, we transcend.

As shadows blend with the falling light,
Echoes guide us through the night.
In every pause, there's depth and grace,
In the quiet, I find your trace.

Together we weave a tapestry bright,
Echoes stitching day into night.
In the stillness, I hear your heart,
A melody where we never part.

Seasons of Comradeship

In springtime's bloom, we find our way,
Laughter dances, bright as day.
Friendships forged in sunlit glow,
Together we rise, together we grow.

Summer whispers secrets shared,
Beneath the stars, we show we cared.
Long nights filled with dreams and fire,
Kindred spirits, lifting higher.

Autumn brings a carpet gold,
Stories told and hands to hold.
As leaves drift down, we cherish past,
In every moment, memories cast.

Winter's chill may wrap us tight,
But hearts unite in cozy light.
Through storms and snow, we stay as one,
Seasons change, our bond not done.

In every turn, through time we roam,
With comradeship, we find our home.
Together through each passing year,
In every moment, love draws near.

Cherished Echoes

Whispers of laughter fill the air,
Memories linger, beyond compare.
In quiet corners, we reminisce,
Moments cherished, wrapped in bliss.

Time flows gently, like a stream,
Carrying echoes of every dream.
Reflections sparkle, hearts entwined,
In cherished echoes, love we find.

Sunlight dances on the wall,
Each shadow tells a story small.
In every heartbeat, a song we sing,
Cherished echoes, a gift we bring.

As seasons change and days unfold,
We weave our tales in threads of gold.
In the tapestry of every hour,
Cherished echoes, love's true power.

Forever held in fragile grace,
In recollection, we find our place.
With every memory, a gentle sigh,
Cherished echoes, never goodbye.

Beacon of Belonging

In the distance, a light shines bright,
Guiding us through the darkest night.
With open hearts and arms so wide,
A beacon of belonging, here we bide.

Familiar faces, smiles that glow,
In unity's warmth, our spirits flow.
Together we stand, hand in hand,
In this sacred space, our dreams expand.

Through trials faced, we find our way,
A bond unbroken, come what may.
In laughter shared and tears aligned,
A beacon of belonging, hearts intertwined.

With every step, we build our path,
In kindness shown, escaping wrath.
A tapestry woven with love's own thread,
A beacon of belonging, where we're led.

As stars align in the midnight's hue,
We find our strength in me and you.
For in this light, we always belong,
In unity's song, forever strong.

Veils of Solitude Lifted

In the quiet, shadows play,
Veils of solitude start to sway.
With every breath, a spark ignites,
In shared moments, our hearts take flight.

Through whispered dreams and gentle ties,
Laughter lifts us to the skies.
Each smile exchanged, a barrier breaks,
In the warmth of love, our spirit wakes.

No longer lost in silent fears,
Together we shed our hidden tears.
With every story, a bond is spun,
Veils of solitude, now come undone.

With open arms, we gather near,
In every heartbeat, we draw clear.
For in connection, we find our way,
Veils of solitude fade away.

As dawn breaks bright, we rise anew,
In unity's grace, we find the true.
With every step, we pave the road,
Veils of solitude, a heavy load.

Shadows and Sunshine

In the morning glow so bright,
Shadows dance, take their flight.
Golden beams through branches weave,
Whispers of what we believe.

Twilight casts a softer shade,
Silhouettes in light conveyed.
Memories flicker, play and tease,
Underneath the swaying trees.

Laughter echoes, sweet and clear,
Holding moments we hold dear.
In the dusk, our hearts align,
In the balance, love will shine.

Every day a new embrace,
Finding warmth in every space.
With each shadow, joy is spun,
In life's tapestry, we're one.

Through the storms and through the light,
We will stand, we will unite.
Hand in hand, we find our way,
In shadows deep, we greet the day.

The Ties that Tangle

Threads of life, entwined so tight,
Binding hearts in day and night.
Complex knots that time has spun,
In every battle, love is won.

Tangled hopes and dreams we chase,
Finding joy in every place.
Through the trials, we will grow,
In the chaos, love will show.

Words unspoken, yet they bind,
In the silence, hearts can find.
Strength in every tear we shed,
Together, in this path we tread.

Each connection, fragile strand,
Woven tightly, hand in hand.
Facing storms that come our way,
In tangle, we choose to stay.

Like the roots beneath the ground,
In the struggle, strength is found.
Through the knots and every tie,
Together, we will always fly.

Chronicles of Togetherness

In a world that turns so fast,
We find peace that's meant to last.
Moments shared like scattered seeds,
Growing strong from little needs.

Seasons change, the stories flow,
In our hearts, the love will grow.
From laughter's light to sorrow's depth,
In our bond, we take each step.

Every chapter tells our tale,
Through the storms, we set our sail.
In the quiet, in the loud,
Hand in hand, we feel so proud.

Through the years, we build our dream,
Every tear, a shining beam.
Together in the dark and light,
In unity, we find our might.

Looking back, our hearts alight,
In the journey, futures bright.
Chronicles of love we penned,
In this dance, there's no end.

Notes from the Heart

Gentle whispers, notes of grace,
Ink of love on every page.
Heartbeats echo, soft and sweet,
In this melody, we meet.

Verses written in the stars,
Carried with us, near and far.
Each line tells a sacred truth,
In the bloom of tender youth.

Songs of joy, notes of sorrow,
Promises of a bright tomorrow.
From the depths, our voices rise,
In the harmony, love defies.

With every breath, the story flows,
In the quiet, love still grows.
Through the struggles, we compose,
Beautiful notes, as life bestows.

So let the heart's song ever play,
In every moment, night or day.
Together, let our spirits dance,
In the music, there's romance.

Bonds Beyond Measure

In the quiet of dusk we stand,
Sharing dreams that weave like sand.
Every laugh a thread of light,
In the shadows, we find our might.

Through storms and trials, we remain,
With hearts entwined, we'll share the pain.
Each moment shapes our story true,
Together, there's nothing we can't do.

Time may bend, but we will grow,
Like rivers strong, and seeds we sow.
In every glance, a silent vow,
Bound forever, here and now.

Through laughter's echo and sorrow's grace,
In every beat, I find yourface.
A bond unyielding, fierce, and pure,
In each other, we find our cure.

With each chapter, new tales unfold,
Yet our connection stays bold.
Like endless skies in sapphire hue,
Always and forever, just us two.

Chronicles of Companionship

Every tale begins with a spark,
A moment shared, igniting the dark.
In laughter's dance, we find our song,
Together, we brave where we belong.

Through seasons change, we walk we'll stride,
In silent whispers, side by side.
The bonds we share, strong like the sea,
A tapestry rich, just you and me.

In the pages worn by time's embrace,
Memory's touch leaves a warm trace.
Each story told, a treasure kept,
With every word, the promise leapt.

We find solace in shared delight,
In darkest hours, we are each light.
A friendship forged through tears and cheers,
In every journey, we calm all fears.

As chapters close, new adventures call,
With unwavering hearts, we dare to fall.
Together we'll write, with ink of gold,
A chronicle of companionship, bold.

Threads of Kindred Spirits

In the fabric of life, we stitch our dreams,
Woven together, or so it seems.
With every thread, a story spins,
In the tapestry, our journey begins.

Through colors bright and shadows cast,
In this artful dance, we've found our past.
With hands held tight, we brave the fray,
In the loom of time, we find our way.

Every whisper that flows from the heart,
In silken tones, we play our part.
Like stars above that softly gleam,
Your spirit shines in every dream.

Though paths may wander, we'll not divide,
In the seams of fate, we're forever tied.
Together we'll paint the sky anew,
With every horizon calling us through.

As seasons change and shadows grow,
In threads of kindness, our love will flow.
Rich as the earth, strong as the sea,
In this fabric, it's you and me.

Whispers in the Wind

In gentle breezes, secrets flow,
Soft like petals, touched by snow.
In the silence, our hearts converse,
With whispers sweet, we softly immerse.

Through fields of dreams, we wander free,
Echoes of laughter, just you and me.
Each moment a gift, each breath a song,
In this sacred space, we belong.

As twilight sets, the stars appear,
An orchestra of love we hold dear.
With every heartbeat, the night unfolds,
Whispers of stories waiting to be told.

Beneath the moon's watchful gaze,
In the soft glow, our spirits blaze.
With every sigh that dances near,
Whispers of connection we hold dear.

As dawn awakens, and night bids farewell,
In every wind's hush, our hearts swell.
A symphony of love that's understood,
In whispers timeless, we find our good.

Growing Together

In the garden of dreams, we sow,
With each passing season, love will grow.
Roots intertwine beneath the earth,
A bond forged in laughter, joy, and mirth.

Through storms that may come, we stand strong,
In harmony, we find where we belong.
Every challenge faced, hand in hand,
Together we flourish, a united band.

Sunshine brings warmth, rain helps us thrive,
In this shared journey, we feel alive.
Petals of hope reach for the sky,
Growing together, you and I.

As time flows gently, like a stream,
We nurture the dreams that fill our theme.
Side by side, through thick and thin,
In the heart's embrace, we both begin.

From tiny seeds, a legacy blooms,
In every corner, love consumes.
Growing together, hearts in sync,
With every moment, we boldly think.

Fellow Travelers on Life's Road

Together we walk this winding path,
Facing the chaos, sharing the laugh.
With every step, stories unfold,
A treasure trove that we will hold.

Under the stars, we share our dreams,
Navigating life's intricate streams.
Through valleys low and mountains high,
With courage and love, we learn to fly.

Through sunny days and darkened nights,
We find our way with newfound sights.
In every heartbeat, there's a song,
A melody of where we belong.

Fellow travelers, hand in hand,
Together we'll conquer, together we stand.
Embracing moments, both big and small,
In the journey of life, we'll have it all.

With laughter as our guiding light,
We weave our tales, shining bright.
In a world diverse, we find our place,
Fellow travelers, we share this space.

A Canvas of Cherished Times

On this canvas, memories paint,
Brushstrokes of laughter, colors quaint.
Each moment captured, a story to tell,
In the gallery of hearts where we dwell.

With hues of joy and shades of tears,
We craft a masterpiece through the years.
Every stroke a testament of love,
A gift from the heavens, shining above.

In the quiet corners, we find our muse,
In the symphony of life, we choose.
Fragments entwined in a tapestry bright,
A canvas evolving, day into night.

As seasons change, our art will grow,
In the warmth of friendship, we sow.
Eternal beauty, our hearts forever twined,
A canvas of cherished times, refined.

In every heartbeat, the colors collide,
With passion and purpose, we won't divide.
Together we paint our dreams sublime,
A canvas adorned with cherished times.

Stars Aligned

In the vast expanse, our paths emerge,
With whispers of fate, we gently surge.
Under the night sky, our dreams ignite,
As if the stars aligned, pure delight.

In cosmic dance, our souls connect,
A tapestry woven with love, respect.
Through trials faced, we find our way,
With every heartbeat, come what may.

Like constellations, we light the dark,
Painting our futures with every spark.
In the universe's embrace, we thrive,
With hearts alight, we truly arrive.

As wishes drift upon the breeze,
In the tranquility, we find our ease.
Together we shine, two hearts entwined,
Guided by destiny, stars aligned.

In every glance, a universe unfolds,
A bond everlasting, more precious than gold.
Together we'll journey, come what may,
With love as our compass, leading the way.

A Symphony of Two

In the hush of twilight's glow,
Soft notes begin to flow,
Heartbeats join the gentle sound,
In harmony, our love is found.

Fingers dance on strings of fate,
Each whisper, a promise great,
Together we create a song,
Where every note can't be wrong.

Eyes meet in the evening light,
In silence, our souls take flight,
A melody that builds anew,
Crafted by a symphony of two.

Through the storms and through the calm,
We weave our lives, a soothing balm,
With every rhythm, every rhyme,
Together we transcend all time.

As stars twinkle in the night,
We sway, beneath their gentle light,
In this dance, we both shall know,
A love that always seems to grow.

Sentinels of Joy

In laughter, we find our way,
Every moment, bright as day,
Guardians of the simple smile,
We share our joy, mile by mile.

With every sunrise, hearts expand,
Together, we make our stand,
In the garden of laughter's bloom,
We chase away all shades of gloom.

Through trials, we learn to cope,
In friendship, we find our hope,
For each tear that rolls in grief,
We meet it with love, our belief.

In the glow of shared delight,
We illuminate the night,
Sentinels of joy, we declare,
In every moment, we are there.

Hand in hand, we carry on,
With songs of peace, the fears are gone,
In unity, our spirits fly,
Together, we touch the sky.

Lanterns of Understanding

In the dark, we find our spark,
With lanterns that shine in the park,
Flickering lights of empathy,
Guiding us through life's treachery.

Each story told, a flame ignites,
Illuminating shared heights,
Through whispers of the heart and soul,
Our differences make us whole.

With every word, a bridge we build,
A tapestry of feelings filled,
Threads of care in every line,
A testament of hearts in time.

Together, we learn and grow,
In understanding, love will glow,
As lanterns flicker in the night,
We walk towards the morning light.

Compassion blooms along the road,
In unity, we share the load,
With every step, we hold the hand,
Of kindness, ever so grand.

Bonds that Bridge

Across the rivers, vast and wide,
We find the paths where hopes abide,
Bonds that bridge the distance near,
Connecting hearts, dispelling fear.

With every challenge that we face,
We weave a tapestry with grace,
In laughter's echo and tears fall,
United, we shall stand tall.

No word unspoken, nor look unseen,
In our embrace, all life's serene,
Foundations built on trust and care,
In every moment, always there.

Through storms and sunlight, we will roam,
With love as our eternal home,
Binding souls and dreams with pride,
In this journey, side by side.

As seasons change and time does flow,
We cherish the bonds that only grow,
In a world that shifts and bends,
Together, we'll be lifelong friends.

The Tapestry of Our Days

Threads of gold and silver sway,
In the quiet light of day.
Whispers weave through every seam,
Stitching together hopes that gleam.

Memories like colors blend,
Intricate patterns that extend.
Laughter echoes in each fold,
Stories waiting to be told.

Fingers tracing patterns fine,
Every moment, love's design.
Frayed edges tell a tale so true,
Binding me forever to you.

Dreams entwined in every hue,
Crafting life anew with you.
In this tapestry, we find,
A glimpse of hearts that are aligned.

Unseen Atlas

Mapping journeys in our minds,
Every twist, a path that binds.
Mountains rise where shadows loom,
Guiding us through darkened room.

Oceans stretch beyond our sight,
Carrying dreams into the night.
With each step, our spirits soar,
On this atlas we explore.

Hidden valleys, forests deep,
Secrets that the world can keep.
Yet within, the compass turns,
For the fire of hope still burns.

Every heartbeat marks a place,
In this vast, unseen embrace.
Together on this endless quest,
Finding solace, finding rest.

A map of hearts, forever drawn,
In the light of every dawn.
With each new path, we learn and grow,
In this journey, love will flow.

Lighthouses in Life

Standing tall against the storm,
Guiding ships, keeping them warm.
A beacon of hope shines so bright,
Illuminating darkest night.

Waves may crash, and winds may howl,
Yet still we hear the lighthouses call.
With every flash, they point the way,
To harbor safe where dreams can stay.

In turbulent seas, we find our guide,
Through shifting tides, they stand with pride.
With hearts aflame, their light shines clear,
Showing love is always near.

Together we sail through tempest's rage,
Finding solace at every page.
In the books of life, we write our fate,
With lighthouses strong, we navigate.

Each guiding light, a story unfolds,
Of love and courage, traditions old.
Together we rise as the waves subside,
In this journey, love is our guide.

Moments in Harmony

In the dance of time we sway,
Melodies whisper in their play.
Hearts in rhythm, side by side,
In every note, our spirits glide.

Sunset paints the sky in gold,
Stories of memories unfold.
In the stillness, we breathe in deep,
Moments cherished, ours to keep.

Like the rustle of leaves in spring,
Every heartbeat finds its ring.
Harmony hums a sweet refrain,
Binding us through joy and pain.

With every glance, a silent song,
In this world, we both belong.
Together weaving threads so fine,
Creating moments, love divine.

In the tapestry of life, we find,
Echoes of hearts, forever aligned.
A symphony that's always true,
Moments in harmony with you.

The Canvas of Us

In hues of laughter, we paint,
A tapestry of dreams so bright.
With every brush, we create,
Memories that fill the night.

The sky above, a blend of stars,
Reflects the stories that we share.
With every stroke, we find our way,
Together, woven without a care.

Each color speaks of moments sweet,
The warmth of sun, the cool of rain.
In this canvas, our hearts meet,
Binding us in joy and pain.

With every shade that comes alive,
We find new paths on this vast space.
Together, we continue to strive,
In this art, we find our place.

Our canvas, ever-changing, flows,
A living piece of love's embrace.
In this art, our spirit grows,
Forever etched in time and space.

Mosaic of Memories

Shattered pieces, bright and bold,
Each moment crafted with great care.
In every tile, stories told,
Fragments of laughter fill the air.

Colors meld in perfect time,
Each memory forms a grand design.
Together, we build the rhyme,
In this mosaic, hearts align.

From joyous nights to quiet days,
Every shard, a part of us.
In this art, we see our ways,
Trust and love, forever a must.

As life's challenges come and go,
We piece together what we find.
In every turn, our spirits glow,
A testament to ties that bind.

This mosaic thrives through storms and sun,
An ever-evolving tale of grace.
In unity, we've truly won,
Creating beauty in this space.

Ties that Bind

Like threads that weave through time and space,
We find a bond that's strong and true.
With each shared laugh, our hearts embrace,
These ties that bind, connect me to you.

Through trials faced, we stand as one,
In every shadow, there's a light.
Together, we've only just begun,
This journey's filled with pure delight.

In moments small, our love expands,
With whispered words and gentle hands.
Across the miles, together we stand,
Through every storm, our hearts command.

Each memory is a sturdy link,
In this chain, we find our way.
Our love, a ship that will not sink,
Navigating life's vast bay.

These ties, unbreakable and bright,
Guide us through both joy and strife.
In every dawn, in every night,
Together, we celebrate this life.

Unbreakable Connections

With every heartbeat, bonds grow tight,
A thread of love that won't unwind.
In this dance, our souls take flight,
In moments shared, our hearts aligned.

Through laughter, tears, the years unfold,
Each memory a cornerstone.
In stories shared, both shy and bold,
Our union thrives, forever grown.

When shadows loom and doubts arise,
We find our strength in one another.
With open hearts and honest sighs,
Together, we uncover cover.

These connections forged in fire,
Unyielding through the trials we face.
In unity, we find our desire,
Together, we embrace our space.

Hand in hand, we walk the road,
With every step, our paths entwine.
In love's embrace, we bear the load,
These unbreakable bonds define.

Souls on the Same Path

In twilight's glow, we find our way,
Two hearts as one, come what may.
Through shadows cast by doubt and fear,
Together we walk, so close, so near.

With every step, the world unfolds,
Stories of life, both new and old.
Hand in hand, we face the dawn,
Two souls entwined, forever drawn.

The whispers of the winds so sweet,
Guide our journey, our hearts' heartbeat.
In laughter shared and tears embraced,
On this path, our strength is traced.

Each challenge met, we rise anew,
Unity blooms in shades of blue.
Through storms that rage and skies so clear,
Our spirits soar, my dear, my dear.

In every twist, a lesson learned,
With every page, the fire burned.
Together, we forge a love so bright,
Souls on the same path, chasing the light.

Bridging the Distance

Across the miles, we cast a line,
Two hearts that beat, a love divine.
Though space may stretch, our bond stays strong,
In dreams we dance, where we belong.

The stars align to light our way,
Guiding our thoughts, night and day.
In whispered words, we find our home,
Together in spirit, never alone.

The ocean's roar, the mountains high,
Can't sever the ties that we rely.
Through letters penned and voices clear,
Bridging the distance, I feel you near.

With every challenge, we learn to trust,
Our faith in love, an unyielding must.
Through time and space, we find a way,
In every heartbeat, come what may.

So let the winds take our dreams far,
For love will always be our star.
Through every journey, I'm with you still,
Bridging the distance, united in will.

Palette of Shared Dreams

In a world of colors, we paint our fate,
With every hue, our hearts create.
A canvas wide, our dreams unfurl,
In vibrant strokes, we change the world.

Gold for laughter, blue for tears,
Each shade holds stories of our years.
With brushes light and spirits high,
We craft our vision, you and I.

The reds and greens of hopes abound,
In swirls and patterns, love is found.
Together we flourish, colors bright,
A masterpiece born from shared light.

As seasons change, our palette too,
Evolves with time, in every view.
Through soft pastels and bold, deep glows,
In every layer, our garden grows.

In this creation, we find our way,
Each stroke reminding us to stay.
Together we blend, like sunlit streams,
In this canvas vast, our shared dreams.

Heartfelt Reflections

In quiet moments, thoughts arise,
Reflections deep, beneath the skies.
With every heartbeat, I feel you near,
Your essence lingers, ever clear.

The mirror shows more than just a face,
It captures love, a warm embrace.
Through time's traversal, we learn and grow,
In heartfelt whispers, our spirits flow.

Each memory woven, a tapestry fine,
Threads of our lives, so closely entwined.
Through stormy days and sunlit streams,
In quiet hours, we share our dreams.

With every tear, and laughter shared,
In moments fragile, true love bared.
Heartfelt reflections, our souls aligned,
In every glance, our purpose defined.

As shadows fade, and daylight breaks,
We find ourselves in every mistake.
In the beauty of this life we weave,
Heartfelt reflections teach us to believe.

Adventures in Unity

Together we roam, hand in hand,
Across the valleys, over the sand.
With laughter and joy in every stride,
Side by side, there's nothing to hide.

Mountains we climb, rivers we cross,
In unity's strength, there's never loss.
Each step we take, a story unfolds,
In the tapestry woven, our journey holds.

Through whispers of night, we share our dreams,
Under the stars, as soft moonlight gleams.
Together we laugh, together we cry,
In this adventure, just you and I.

In every challenge, we find our grace,
In each other's eyes, a warm embrace.
The world is vast, yet we are free,
In unity's heart, we shall always be.

With open hearts, we bravely explore,
In every moment, there's so much more.
Our adventures in unity, forever bright,
Together we shine, like stars in the night.

Reflections of Togetherness

In quiet moments, side by side,
We share our thoughts, our hearts open wide.
Each word we speak, a gentle caress,
In the warmth of togetherness, we find our rest.

Through every season, hand in hand,
We create memories, like grains of sand.
With every smile, every sigh,
In reflections of love, our spirits fly.

In laughter and tears, we journey deep,
In the bonds we forge, our secrets keep.
Through the storms that may come, we stand strong,
In the song of togetherness, we belong.

In the dance of life, our steps align,
In every heartbeat, your soul meets mine.
With every challenge, we rise anew,
In reflections of togetherness, we break through.

As dawn unfolds, the world awakes,
With shared hopes and dreams, our path we make.
In the light of love, we shine so bright,
In reflections of togetherness, we find our light.

A Dance of Souls

Two spirits entwined in a graceful sway,
In the rhythm of time, we find our way.
With every heartbeat, a new song plays,
In this dance of souls, forever we stay.

Under the moonlight, we twirl and glide,
In the silence of night, our hearts confide.
With whispered secrets in every twine,
A dance of souls, perfectly aligned.

Through seasons changing, our steps remain,
In the laughter and joy, in sunshine and rain.
We embrace the music, both tender and bold,
In this dance of souls, our story is told.

With every spin, we weave our fate,
In the warmth of your touch, I hesitate.
Together we flow, like rivers meet sea,
In this dance of souls, just you and me.

As the world fades, we rise and fall,
In the harmony of love, we have it all.
With every moment captured in time,
In the dance of souls, our hearts climb.

Shared Sunsets

As day turns to night, we stand in awe,
Watching the colors, without a flaw.
In the gold and pink, a story unfolds,
In shared sunsets, our love is told.

With whispered wishes, we send them high,
As the sun bows low in the evening sky.
Hand in hand, we breathe the glow,
In the warmth of the moment, our hearts overflow.

The horizon stretches, a canvas divine,
In every heartbeat, your soul meets mine.
With the stars as witnesses, we find our way,
In shared sunsets, we choose to stay.

In the stillness of dusk, our dreams ignite,
In the fading light, our spirits take flight.
With every sunset, new hopes arise,
In shared sunsets, we reach for the skies.

As the sky darkens, we hold on tight,
In the promise of tomorrow, love shines bright.
With every evening, a love song plays,
In shared sunsets, forever we gaze.

Stories Woven in Time

In the quiet hours, tales arise,
Whispers of old beneath the skies.
Memories stitched with threads of gold,
Each moment cherished, a treasure to hold.

Through laughter and tears, we weave our fate,
The fabric of life, intricate and great.
Every story shared, a bond to find,
In the tapestry of hearts intertwined.

Stars guide our paths in the night,
Illuminating dreams, shining bright.
Past and present, forever entwined,
Echoes of stories in hearts and minds.

Seasons change, yet tales remain,
Carved in time, through joy and pain.
Together we grow, together we learn,
Through stories told, bright embers burn.

Listen closely, to the winds that sigh,
Each whispers a truth, a reason why.
In every journey, in every climb,
We find ourselves, stories woven in time.

Touchstones of Kindness

In gentle gestures, kindness shines,
A smile exchanged, the heart entwines.
With open hands, we lift each other,
In every soul, a sister or brother.

A helping hand in the darkest night,
A word of comfort, a beacon of light.
Small acts of care, they gently grow,
Blooming in hearts, the warmth we know.

Kindness whispers in the breeze,
A soothing touch, like rustling leaves.
Through storms we stand, united and strong,
In the embrace of love, we all belong.

Moments shared, in laughter and tears,
Comforting presence calms our fears.
With every deed, we make the world bright,
Touchstones of kindness, our guiding light.

In the tapestry of life we weave,
Every thread of kindness believes.
Together we rise, together we find,
The beauty of hearts, endlessly kind.

Harmony in Diversity

Colors united, a vibrant parade,
Voices of many, a song is played.
In every heartbeat, differences blend,
Strength in variety, we comprehend.

Cultures entwined, together we dance,
Every step helps us take a chance.
With open minds, we learn and grow,
In the garden of life, seeds we sow.

Bridges of hope in every embrace,
Respecting each story, each unique face.
With love as the key, we unlock the door,
Harmony thrives, forevermore.

Voices together, a beautiful sound,
In unity's strength, hope is found.
Hand in hand, we rise and thrive,
Celebrating the colors that keep us alive.

Let's cherish the difference, let's stand as one,
In the tapestry of life, we've just begun.
Together we sing, together we strive,
In this harmony, we truly arrive.

Challenges Shared

In the face of struggle, we hold the line,
Sharing the burdens, your hand in mine.
Through trials faced, we gather our might,
Together we shine, turning dark into light.

With every setback, we learn to rise,
Finding strength in each other's eyes.
A woven path of empathy clear,
In moments shared, we conquer fear.

The weight lessens when kindness flows,
In unity's heart, resilience grows.
Facing the storms, we stand as one,
With shared love and hope, battles are won.

Hearts united, we face the tide,
In the journey together, we take pride.
The challenges faced, a chance to grow,
In the warmth of community, strength will show.

Through every hardship, we build and mend,
In the tapestry of life, love will transcend.
Together we rise, come what may,
In challenges shared, we find our way.

In the Embrace of Friendship

In laughter's echo, bonds are sealed,
Through quiet moments, hearts revealed.
Together we stand, come joy or strife,
In the embrace of friendship, we find life.

Shared secrets whispered, trust that's deep,
In every promise, a vow we keep.
Through storms and sunshine, side by side,
In the embrace of friendship, we confide.

Paths intertwined, like roots of a tree,
Nurtured by love, wild and free.
In every journey, memories blend,
In the embrace of friendship, time won't end.

Hands held tightly, warmth in the night,
In silent understanding, everything's right.
With every heartbeat, we rise and fall,
In the embrace of friendship, we have it all.

Through laughter and tears, our spirits soar,
In every moment, we crave for more.
With every glance, a tale is spun,
In the embrace of friendship, we've already won.

The Soul's Mirror

In your gaze, I see my truth,
A reflection of dreams and youth.
The whispers of wisdom, softly shared,
In the soul's mirror, we are laid bare.

Every smile, a spark divine,
In your laughter, I hear the sign.
Cleansing shadows, revealing light,
In the soul's mirror, all feels right.

With every heartbeat, we draw near,
In our silence, we share the fear.
Yet through the pain, our spirits mend,
In the soul's mirror, we transcend.

Through trials faced, our bonds will grow,
With every truth, our colors show.
In moments cherished, we find the prize,
In the soul's mirror, love never lies.

Hand in hand, our essence blends,
In unity's warmth, the journey bends.
Together we shine, a radiant hue,
In the soul's mirror, it's me and you.

Eternal Flames

In the dark, our lights ignite,
Two souls dancing, hearts take flight.
Through time's embrace, we softly sway,
Eternal flames, lighting the way.

With every glance, a fire grows,
In every touch, a warmth that glows.
Together we burn, fierce and bright,
Eternal flames, a guiding light.

Through stormy nights and endless days,
In passion's blaze, we find our ways.
In whispered secrets, dreams we share,
Eternal flames light up the air.

Hand in hand, our spirits soar,
In every moment, we crave for more.
Through trials faced, our love remains,
Eternal flames, through joys and pains.

In the quiet, our hearts chant,
A symphony of love, an endless grant.
Together forever, as life reclaims,
Eternal flames, where passion names.

Light in Each Other's Eyes

In the dawn's glow, our spark ignites,
Two souls entwined in gentle sights.
A promise whispered, soft and clear,
Light in each other's eyes, we steer.

Every heartbeat, a rhythm so true,
In every glance, I find my cue.
With every laugh, joy multiplies,
Light in each other's eyes, a prize.

Through shadows cast, we find the warmth,
In shared moments, love's true form.
With open hearts, we face the skies,
Light in each other's eyes, love flies.

Each step we take, a dance divine,
In the story woven, stars align.
Through every trial, we rise and rise,
Light in each other's eyes, never dies.

In the twilight, as dreams unfold,
In the quietude, our futures told.
With every sigh, our spirits tie,
Light in each other's eyes, we fly.

Footprints in the Sand

As the tide pulls away, softly it reveals,
Moments we shared, a dance of many seals.
Each grain of sand speaks, whispers in the breeze,
Echoes of laughter, drifting with such ease.

Under the sun, where the waves gently kiss,
Memories linger, a fleeting, warm bliss.
Footprints left behind, washed away with time,
Yet in my heart, they forever will chime.

A journey we took, with shadows to lead,
Together we walked, in moments we'd freed.
The ocean, a witness to dreams that we planned,
Forever connected, like footprints in sand.

The evening draws close, the waters recede,
Still we remember the love that we need.
In twilight's embrace, where the stars take their stand,
We cherish the echoes, like footprints in sand.

As night falls upon us, the sky cloaked in dark,
We carry the symbols that keep us from stark.
Each wave that rolls in brings a heartfelt demand,
To treasure our journey, like footprints in sand.

The Gift of Shared Stories

Gathered around, warm flames in the night,
Tales weave like threads, in the soft, golden light.
Voices intertwine, laughter hangs in the air,
Each story a treasure, beyond compare.

In the silence that follows, a heartbeat is felt,
Memories painted, where joy was once dealt.
With each whispered word, we bind our hearts tight,
The gift of shared stories, a profound delight.

From misty beginnings to journeys anew,
Every tale reflects not just me, but you.
In the ink of our lives, we find who we are,
Bound by the fibers, that twinkle like stars.

As night stretches onward, the tales start to blend,
Each ending a promise, each message a friend.
In the warmth of connection, we're never alone,
The gift of shared stories, a love built on stone.

When the fire's glow fades, and the night turns to grey,
These stories remain, lighting up our way.
Forever we'll carry the words that ignite,
The gift of shared stories, our beacon of light.

Reflections of Us

In the mirror's gaze, a journey unfolds,
Reflections of us, in whispers untold.
Like rivers that flow, our lives intertwine,
In each little glance, our hearts brightly shine.

Moments captured in laughs and in tears,
The story of us spans over the years.
In shadows of dusk, our images dance,
Reflections of love, built from chance.

With every sunrise, new colors appear,
Painting the canvas of dreams we hold dear.
A mosaic of moments, both large and small,
Reflections of us, the rise and the fall.

In twilight's embrace, where silence reveals,
The echoes of laughter, the softness it heals.
Bound by the memories, like stars in the sky,
Reflections of us, they never will die.

Through trials and joys, through darkness and light,
Together we shine, like the moon in the night.
In these gentle reflections, we discover our truth,
Forever in tune with the rhythm of youth.

Lanterns in the Dark

In the depths of night, where shadows take flight,
Lanterns flicker softly, casting warm light.
Guiding our paths, through the silence we roam,
Each glow tells a story, leading us home.

With whispers of hope, the darkness retreats,
Each lantern a promise, where cold heartbeats meet.
Together we wander, through fears we embark,
Illuminating dreams, like lanterns in dark.

In the stillness we find, the strength to believe,
That even in shadows, it's light we conceive.
With hands joined as one, we banish the stark,
Creating a forest of lanterns in dark.

As dawn starts to break, the night slowly fades,
Yet memories linger in soft, gentle shades.
Our lanterns will flicker, in hearts that we park,
Forever kindled, like lanterns in dark.

Through trials we face, together we stand,
With love as our lantern, we'll light up the land.
In the tapestry woven from journeys we embark,
Together forever, like lanterns in dark.

Conversations in Color

Whispers painted in hues of light,
Brushstrokes dance, a vivid sight.
Words flow like rivers, swift and bold,
In every shade, our stories unfold.

Crimson cheer and cerulean grace,
Each tone, a memory we embrace.
In laughter's laughter, the skies ignite,
Conversations bloom, a kaleidoscope bright.

Emerald dreams as we intertwine,
With every heartbeat, you are mine.
Golden moments in twilight's glow,
Color our lives, forever aglow.

Pastels whisper secrets untold,
In friendship's warmth, we'll never fold.
Through shadows and light, we weave our art,
Forever connected, heart to heart.

In every canvas, we leave our mark,
A tapestry woven, from light to dark.
Conversations flutter like wings of a dove,
In this world of color, we find our love.

Alliances of the Heart

In twilight's glow, two souls align,
A pact unspoken, pure and divine.
Through trials and joy, we find our way,
Alliances forged, come what may.

Hand in hand, we face each storm,
In the warmth of us, our hearts stay warm.
With whispered hopes, we share the weight,
Together we stand, defying fate.

In laughter's echo, our spirits soar,
Every heartbeat speaks, forevermore.
Threads of connection, woven so tight,
An unbreakable bond, shining bright.

Through valleys low and peaks so high,
In every moment, you and I.
The journey unfolds, side by side,
In love's embrace, we'll always abide.

With dreams like lanterns, lighting our way,
In the tapestry of life, we play.
Alliances of the heart, a sacred art,
Two souls united, never apart.

The Song of Shared Dreams

In the quiet night, our dreams take flight,
Melodies woven, a beautiful sight.
Harmonies rise, laughter entwined,
In the song of us, true love defined.

Each note a whisper, soft and sweet,
Together we dance, hearts skip a beat.
In twilight's embrace, visions unfold,
Stories of love, forever retold.

Stars above shimmer, guiding our way,
In the chorus of hope, we choose to stay.
With hearts wide open, we sing along,
Creating a legacy, a timeless song.

Every dream shared, a treasure we find,
In the rhythm of life, two hearts aligned.
From dusk until dawn, through joy and strife,
In the song we sing, we find our life.

Together we'll soar, let the music play,
In the symphony of love, we'll always stay.
The song of shared dreams, a beautiful thread,
In the fabric of time, our hearts are wed.

Echoes of You and Me

In every moment, echoes softly call,
Whispers of you bounce off the wall.
In shadows of laughter, we find our trace,
Memories linger, a warm embrace.

Days flow like rivers, swift and true,
In every heartbeat, we come into view.
Time may wander, but love will stay,
Echoes of us, lighting the way.

Through storms we weather, hand in hand,
In the echoes, we make our stand.
With every sunrise, a promise anew,
In the silence, it's always you.

Every glance shared, a story's reprise,
In the echoes of love, we rise.
A melody sweet, a timeless refrain,
With every heartbeat, we dance through the rain.

In the quiet hours, we find our song,
In the echoes of you, I forever belong.
Together in whispers, we craft our tale,
Echoes of you and me, love will prevail.

Chronicles of Shared Adventures

In valleys deep, we started our quest,
With maps unrolled, we felt so blessed.
Through mountains high and rivers wide,
Together we faced the rising tide.

With every step, new stories grew,
Of trials faced and triumphs too.
A bond was formed with each sunset,
In memories made, we won't forget.

The laughter shared on long winding roads,
In every town, our joy bestowed.
As night fell soft, we pitched our tents,
In whispered tales, our hearts contents.

Through stormy nights and sunny days,
We wandered free in countless ways.
The call of adventure, a siren's song,
In each new dawn, we felt we belong.

Though paths may part and seasons change,
Our shared adventures will never be strange.
In the chronicles written in stars above,
Lies the essence of our friendship and love.

The Sound of Laughter

In a quiet room, echoes arise,
Laughter dances beneath the skies.
It weaves through whispers, a gentle thread,
Painting joy where shadows tread.

A burst of glee, a contagious cheer,
It bridges the distance, brings us near.
In silly moments, we find delight,
Turning ordinary days into pure light.

With every chuckle, our spirits soar,
A balm for the heart, a joyful roar.
The sound of laughter is a cherished gift,
A spark of happiness, a beautiful lift.

When troubles loom and spirits wane,
In laughter's embrace, we break the chain.
Through ups and downs, it keeps us tight,
A melody of love, shining so bright.

So let the laughter guide the way,
Through all our nights and every day.
For in each giggle, a memory stays,
The sound of laughter, our hearts ablaze.

Companions Under Stars

Beneath a blanket of twinkling light,
We gather close on a quiet night.
With dreams to share, we gaze above,
Through whispered hopes, we feel the love.

The moon casts shadows, soft and bright,
As stories unfold in the cool twilight.
With each passing star, a wish is made,
Friendship sealed in memories laid.

We speak of journeys yet to undertake,
With hearts aligned, there's no mistake.
In this moment, time stands still,
As laughter echoes, hearts we fill.

Companions under the celestial view,
In our shared dreams, a bond so true.
With each illuminating spark we see,
We write our fate, forever free.

When morning comes and the stars retreat,
In our hearts, these memories meet.
For under the stars, we forged our way,
As lifelong companions, come what may.

A Journey Worth Taking

With every step, a new dawn breaks,
In paths untrodden, the heart awakes.
The road ahead stretches wide and clear,
A journey worth taking, year after year.

We set our sights on distant lands,
With open minds and outstretched hands.
The thrill of adventure calls out loud,
As we chase dreams, both humble and proud.

From mountains high to valleys low,
Together we wander, together we grow.
Each twist and turn, a lesson to learn,
With courage ignited, we take our turn.

Through laughter and tears, we'll face the unknown,
In every challenge, our spirits have grown.
For in the journey, we find our place,
A tapestry woven with love and grace.

So here we stand, at the journey's start,
With open souls and an eager heart.
A journey worth taking, hand in hand,
Creating memories that forever stand.

Letters Unwritten

In the shadows, words remain,
Waiting for the ink to flow.
Whispers lost in silent pain,
Echoes of what we will not show.

Pages blank and hearts concealed,
Fears of truth that roam the night.
All my hopes yet to be healed,
In the darkness, seeking light.

Fragile dreams in quiet folds,
Promises that drift like leaves.
Stories yearning to be told,
Yet in silence, sorrow weaves.

Inkless thoughts, a heavy sigh,
Wishes penned but never cast.
Lost between the you and I,
In the future, tied to past.

So here I stand, my heart laid bare,
Holding thoughts I cannot speak.
Longing for the warmth and care,
In letters unwritten, I feel weak.

The Symphony of Us

In the dawn, our voices blend,
A melody that feels like home.
Each note a bond, a message penned,
On this journey, we will roam.

Harmony through stormy skies,
With every beat, our spirits rise.
In the dance, our passion flies,
Together in the dream we size.

Every laugh a sweet refrain,
Every tear a heavy beat.
Each moment holds joy and pain,
In the tempo, our hearts meet.

Through the silence, through the noise,
In every chord, we find our way.
Together we will make the choice,
In this symphony, we will stay.

So join me, love, and take a hand,
Compose the life we wish to pen.
In the music, understand,
Our symphony shall never end.

Together We Soar

In the twilight, we take flight,
Hearts entwined, we leave the ground.
With hope's wings, we chase the light,
In the vastness, joy is found.

Through the clouds, our spirits dance,
Breath of freedom fills our lungs.
In the magic of this chance,
Love's sweet rhythm softly strung.

With every gust, we lift and sway,
The world below now far away.
In the blue, we choose to play,
Together in this bright array.

With open hearts, we dare to dream,
Fearless in our bold ascent.
In laughter's warmth, life's vibrant gleam,
Together strong, we find content.

So let us soar, forever free,
In the sky where love takes hold.
In each other, we will be,
The stories of our hearts retold.

The Garden of Trust

In the quiet, roots entwine,
Nurtured by the light of day.
With each bloom, a love divine,
In the garden, we will stay.

Tender whispers, soft embrace,
Petals fall, then rise again.
In this sacred, cherished space,
Trust grows stronger through the rain.

With every season, we shall learn,
To tend the seeds that we have sown.
Through the trials, hearts will yearn,
In this garden, we have grown.

Vows like vines that intertwine,
Holding fast through storms we face.
In our hearts the sun will shine,
As we navigate this place.

So let us cultivate with care,
The love that blossoms, pure and true.
In the garden, we will share,
A future bright, just me and you.

Kaleidoscope of Trust

In a world where colors blend,
Each hue a promise, we defend.
A bond that shapes our every view,
In every shade, I trust in you.

Through twists and turns, we find our way,
In laughter's glow and shadows' sway.
With every glance, we build a dream,
Our hearts, a flowing silver stream.

As fragments dance in swirling light,
Each moment shared ignites the night.
With open hands, we weave our fate,
A tapestry that can't be late.

In silence speaks a knowing glance,
The world may shift, but we still dance.
Together strong through thick and thin,
In every loss, we still can win.

So let the colors swirl and spin,
With trust our guide, we'll journey in.
No fear can dim our vibrant song,
With hearts united, we belong.

Stargazer's Comrade

Beneath the vast and starry skies,
We whisper dreams, where silence lies.
Your gaze, a beacon in the night,
Together, we embrace the light.

With every twinkle, secrets shared,
A cosmic bond, a love declared.
The universe unfolds so wide,
In you, my endless joy, my guide.

We chase the comets' fleeting tails,
Through endless nights and whispered tales.
With every wish upon a star,
I find my place, no matter far.

Through cosmic storms and shooting stars,
We'll navigate this realm of ours.
In harmony, our spirits soar,
Together, always seeking more.

So let the heavens spark our fate,
As stardust dreams we cultivate.
In every glow, my heart you view,
A stargazer's love, forever true.

Roots Intertwined

In earth's embrace, our futures blend,
With whispered vows, we start to mend.
Roots reaching deep, securing trust,
In every storm, it's love we must.

Through seasons change, our bond holds tight,
In shadows cast, we find the light.
With branches strong, we rise and grow,
Together through the ebb and flow.

Beneath the surface, life abides,
A tapestry where warmth resides.
With every touch, the soil knows,
The love that nurtures, softly grows.

In tangled paths, we learn to share,
A history steeped in tender care.
With every heartbeat, roots entwined,
In love's embrace, our souls aligned.

So let us flourish, side by side,
In nature's grace, our hearts confide.
Together strong, through every climb,
Forever bound in space and time.

Harbor in the Storm

When tempest roars and shadows loom,
I find my peace within your room.
A lighthouse shining through the night,
Your presence is my guiding light.

In raging waves, our hearts collide,
With every swell, we turn the tide.
Through thunder's crash, I hold you near,
In every storm, I find my cheer.

Your arms, a haven from the fray,
In storms of life, we find our way.
With whispered dreams, we brave the night,
Together facing dawn's first light.

No fear can reign when love is true,
In every gale, I'll sail with you.
Through wildest seas, our hearts remain,
A bond unbroken by the rain.

So let the storms come crashing down,
In your embrace, I'll never drown.
With every tide, we'll make it through,
A harbor safe, where love is new.

Bonds of Laughter

In the garden of joy, we play,
Echoes of giggles drift away.
Each memory a colorful hue,
Illuminating skies so blue.

Under the sun, we dance so free,
Together, you and I, just we.
With every chuckle, love's embrace,
A tapestry that time can't erase.

Moments woven in pure delight,
Stars twinkling softly in the night.
A shared joke, a glance we know,
In laughter, our hearts gently glow.

Through trials and storms, laughter binds,
A melody in the heart that finds.
In every chuckle, a story grows,
A hidden magic that only shows.

In bonds of laughter, we remain,
Through sunshine, sorrow, joy, and pain.
A symphony of love so vast,
A treasure we hold, a flag at half-mast.

Threads of Trust

In the quiet, whispers flow,
Woven secrets only we know.
A delicate fabric, strong and true,
Each thread a promise, me and you.

Through storms of doubt, we stand tall,
Building a fortress, we won't fall.
Each glance exchanged, a silent vow,
Bound by trust, here and now.

In shadows deep, our light shines bright,
Guiding each other through the night.
With every heartbeat, courage grows,
In the tapestry of life, it shows.

Threads may fray, but never break,
Through every choice that we make.
A bond unspoken, deep and strong,
In the fabric of trust, we belong.

With every step, our paths entwined,
In the story of us, love defined.
Through winding roads and tangled paths,
Together in trust, we find our laughs.

Companionship Chronicles

In the pages of time, we write,
Adventures taken, stars so bright.
Through laughter and tears, we explore,
Every chapter opens a new door.

From late-night talks to golden days,
In every moment, our spirit plays.
A journey shared, a hand to hold,
In stories of warmth, our hearts are bold.

Through winters cold and summers warm,
Together we weather every storm.
Each memory penned, a joyful spark,
In this chronicle, we leave our mark.

With whispers of dreams and hopes to chase,
In the comfort of each other's space.
Navigating life, side by side,
In the book of companionship, we abide.

Each sunrise brings a brand-new tale,
A shared vision that will not pale.
In the chronicle of hearts aglow,
Together forever, we ebb and flow.

Secrets Shared in Silence

In the hush of night, words fade,
Secrets linger in the shade.
A gentle nod, a knowing glance,
In silent moments, we take a chance.

Through quiet spaces, bonds grow tight,
In the stillness, feels so right.
Each sigh a tale of love and pain,
In the silence, we break the chain.

With whispers soft, our hearts converse,
Hidden stories that we immerse.
In muted gestures, truth takes flight,
Together we paint the darkest night.

In the comfort of unspoken trust,
Every glance holds a world unjust.
A secret language, just we two,
In peaceful silence, I find you.

Each moment shared, a treasure kept,
In the quiet, our souls have leapt.
In secrets shared, we find our way,
In silence, love is here to stay.

Milton Keynes UK
Ingram Content Group UK Ltd.
UKHW022004131124
451149UK00013B/1007